HANNAH
goes with her cat to
The Vet

by Helen and Clive Dorman

Paediatric Consultant:
Dr Huw R Jenkins MA MD FRCP FRCPCH

CP Publishing

Let us say hello to Hannah, the people and the pets she meets at the vet's.

Hello Hannah and Winston!

Hello Sonny, Hattie, Linda and Fionn with Ivy, Scribble and Scoot!

Hello Tina, James and Bodger!

Hello Sheila, Isabelle, and Hoppy!

Hello Susan.
Susan is the veterinary
nurse.

Hello Scott.
Scott is the vet.

Let us turn the pages and find out what happens at the vet's today.

Hannah and her mummy are outside the vet's.
They are carrying a wicker basket. Inside the basket is
Hannah's cat, Winston. Winston is going to the vet for a
check-up. If he is well, the vet is going to fit Winston
with a microchip. The chip has a special number which
works like a name tag.
Winston does not like being away from home but he
feels safer when he is being carried inside the basket.

Inside the vet's there is a waiting room.
The waiting room is where people stay with their pets until the vet is ready to see them. Everyone takes it in turns.
Hattie, Linda and Fionn are sitting down with their guinea pigs, Scribble, Ivy and Scoot.
Sonny sees that the box for the guinea pigs is empty now and he steps inside it to play.

Do you like playing in cardboard boxes?
What games do you play?

Hannah's mummy is checking-in Winston with Susan, the veterinary nurse.
Hannah can just see over the counter!
Winston is hiding in the back of the basket. He does not like the strange smells of other animals in the vet's, or the voices of people he does not know.

Everyone is waiting for their turn to see the vet.
Hannah has not been this close to a guinea pig before
and she is a little worried. Hattie says that Scribble is
very friendly.

Hannah's mummy gently strokes Scribble's nose to
show Hannah it is alright.

Today, the guinea pigs are going to have their claws
clipped by the vet.

Can you count the guinea pigs?

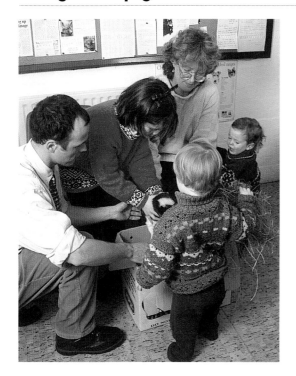

1 Scott the vet helps Hattie put Ivy in the box.

2 Linda shows Fionn that they are all safe.

3 The box is shut.

4 They all go with Scott.

1 Sheila, Isabelle and their rabbit, Hoppy, have also come to see the vet. Today, Hoppy is going to have her teeth checked.

2 Hannah likes rabbits. She and Isabelle both stroke Hoppy.

Where do you go to have your teeth checked?

3 Isabelle lets Hannah have Hoppy on her lap.
Hannah likes Hoppy.

1 Now Tina, James and Bodger have arrived. Hannah and Isabelle have put Hoppy back in his box. Hoppy does not like dogs.

2 Tina asks Hannah and Isabelle if Bodger feels different from Hoppy when they stroke him.

Who do you think is the softest to stroke, Bodger or Hoppy?

3 Hannah asks Tina if Bodger likes children. Tina says he loves them and he is very gentle. Bodger likes the smells of the other animals and he wants to explore the waiting room.

4 Bodger is kept on a lead so that he stays with Tina and James. He may frighten the other animals.

1 It is now Winston's turn to see the vet. Winston has been put on the vet's table. He is still in the basket.

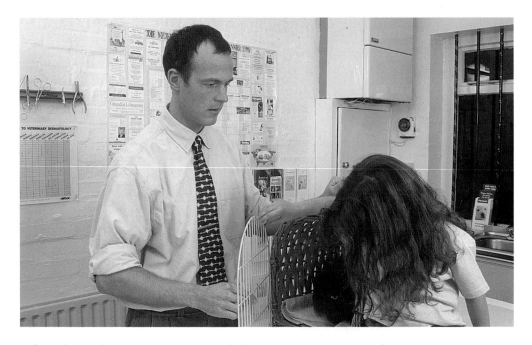

2 The basket is opened but Winston does not want to come out.

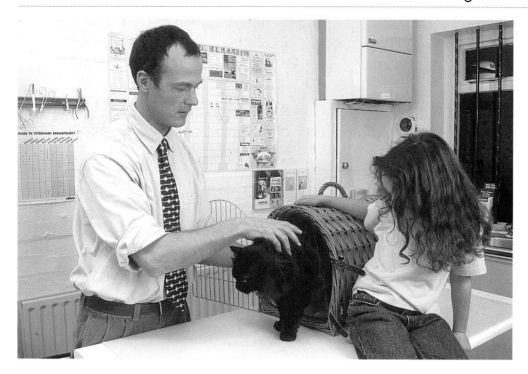

3 Scott gently helps Winston out of the basket.

4 Scott begins to examine Winston to see if he is in good health. Hannah comforts Winston.

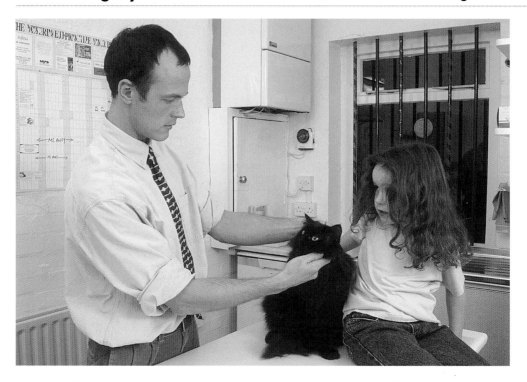

1 Scott looks at Winston's eyes. He makes sure they are clear and bright.

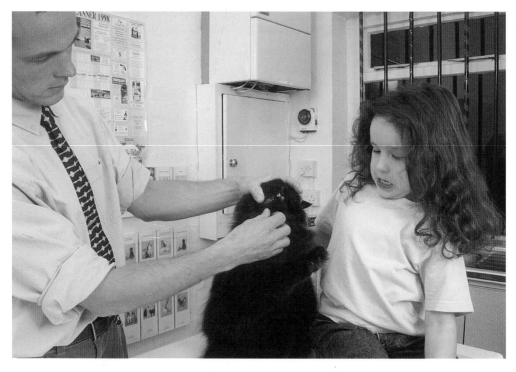

2 Then Winston's teeth. No, not yours, Hannah!

3 Scott feels Winston's back and tummy.
He is finding out if Winston has any pain.

4 Next Scott and Hannah look into his ear.

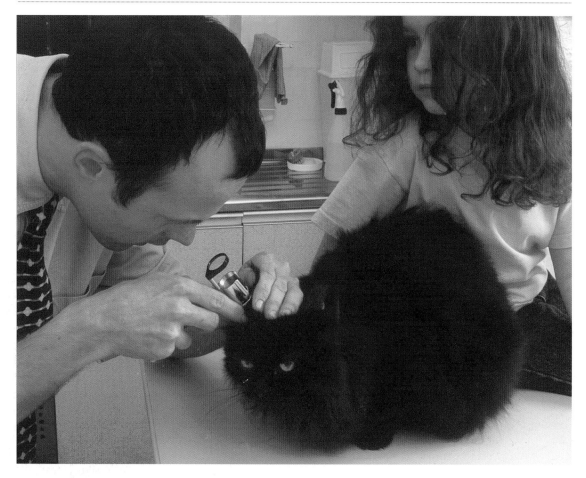

1 Scott has a closer look into Winston's ear.

2 He then takes his
temperature.

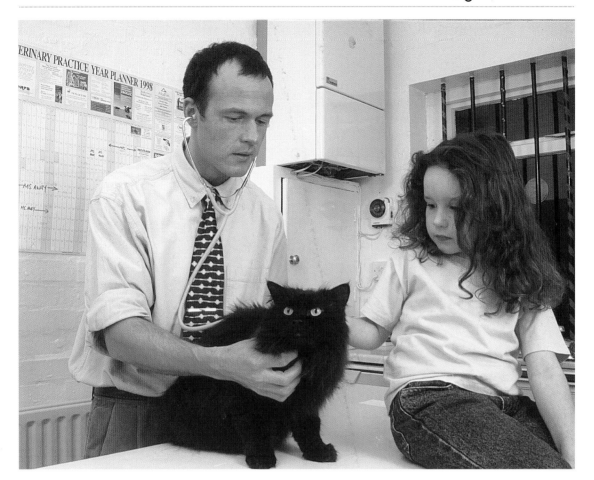

3 Finally Scott listens to Winston's heart with a
stethoscope.
Everything is fine. Winston is a very healthy cat.

Do you know who else uses a stethoscope?

1 Scott can now give Winston an identity microchip.
If Winston ever gets lost, he can be returned home.

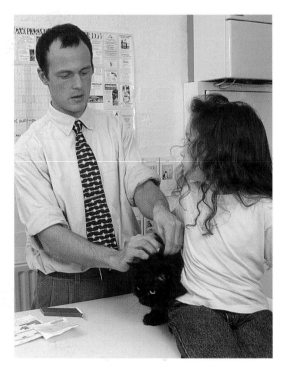

2 Scott cleans the area on
Winston's neck.

3 Then he puts in the chip
under Winston's skin.

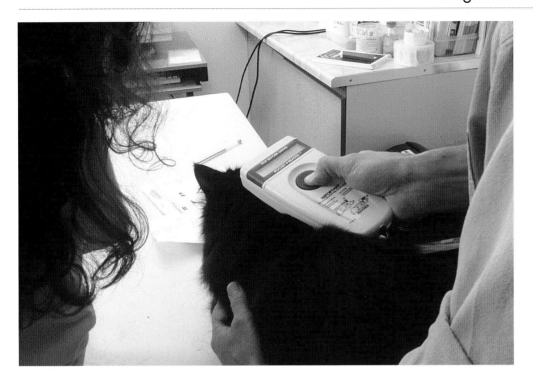

4 Scott tests that the chip works. The chip carries a special number which is only for Winston.

5 The number is written down and kept safely.

6 So is Winston's address.

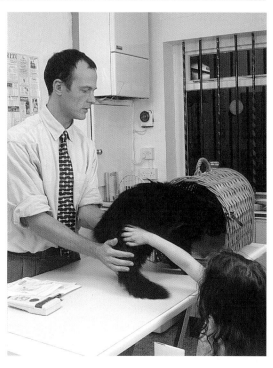

1 Scott gives an envelope to Hannah.

2 Scott and Hannah help Winston into his basket.

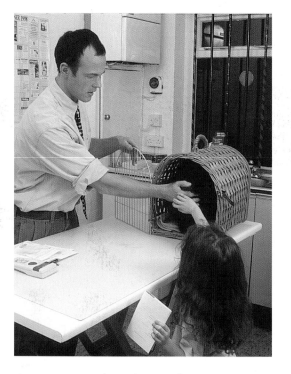

3 Just one last push...

4 Winston is safe inside.

Scott has lifted Winston off the table and is carrying him back into the waiting room.
'Thank you,' says Hannah.

1 Hannah's mummy pays Susan. Hannah is making sure that Winston is happy in his basket.

2 At last it is time to take Winston back home.

Hannah and Winston are back home again. They are happy to be back in the garden.
What an adventure they have had!

Do you think Winston has been a brave cat?
Do you think Hannah has helped Winston today?

Scott says, 'this is how to keep your pet healthy...'

- Give it good food.
- Give it fresh water at all times.
- Give it a clean and warm bed.
- Give it plenty of exercise and lots of love.
- Groom it once a day.
- Check that its ears, eyes and nose are healthy.
- Check that its teeth and claws are not too long.
- If your pet is in a cage, it should be cleaned out at least once a week.

...and remember that a pet is not a furry toy.

What are the animals doing in the pictures?

Scott says, 'observe your pet and get to know it. If your pet shows any of these symptoms you need to take it to the vet...'

- It is not its normal self.
- It sleeps more than usual.
- It is not eating much.
- It is coughing or sneezing.
- It is lame.
- It has sore ears or eyes.
- It seems unhappy.

When you take your pet to the vet's or travel on a journey...

- Carry it in a suitable strong basket or box with airholes.
- Make your pet comfortable with hay, straw or a favourite blanket.
- Give it water on long journeys.
- Make sure it is not too hot or too cold.
- If you *have* to leave your pet in the car, park in the shade with the windows open for air and be as quick as you can.
- Have larger pets microchipped in case they get lost.

Scott says, 'when you go on holiday, find someone to look after your pets'.

Leave a list of jobs that need to be done and the phone number of your vet.

If you move into a new home, give your pets time to settle in.

- There will be lots of new, strange smells for them to get used to.
- Cats should be kept indoors for two weeks to get used to their new home. After that put a lead on your cat and take it out to explore its new surroundings.

Scott says, 'pet's tails help to show us if the animal is happy or cross – they are NOT to be pulled'.

- If a cat's tail is flicking from side to side it is not happy – so leave it alone.
- If a dog wags its tail it is happy.
- When you meet a new dog, always ask the owner if it is friendly. Let the dog sniff the back of your hand before you stroke the dog.

If you find an injured wild animal, call your local RSPCA or animal welfare organisation.
If you find a baby wild animal without its parent you should leave it alone.

Can you name everyone and their pets on these pages?

Bye bye...
and ...

Bye bye... , ... , ... and ... ,
with ... , ... , and ...

Bye bye... , ...
and ...

Bye bye... , ...
and ...

Bye bye...　　　　　　　　Bye bye...

Now it is time to say bye bye to
Hannah and Winston;
Sonny, Hattie, Linda and Fionn with Ivy, Scribble and
Scoot;
Tina, James and Bodger;
Sheila, Isabelle and Hoppy;
and of course Susan, the veterinary nurse
and Scott, the vet.
Bye bye!

The importance of animal care

Owning any pet is a serious commitment and deciding to give a home to one should be discussed by all the family. Pet ownership is for the entire life of the animal and its needs are often time-consuming and can be expensive.

Pets do not need just housing and feeding; there are many other points to consider. Kittens are very active and like to climb and scratch. Puppies like to chew and need patient training, and once grown, a dog should be walked twice a day – even when it is cold, wet and windy! Dogs love company, so if you work, remember it is not good for them to be left on their own for long periods during the day. Vets' fees must be considered – even inoculations can be expensive – and treating a sick or injured animal can be *very* expensive. It may well be worth looking into a pet insurance policy: there are many available to suit your animal's needs.

During a family holiday your pet must be looked after by someone reliable, or boarded at kennels or a cattery, which is another expense. The kennels or cattery will expect to see paperwork of up-to-date vaccinations, and will take an animal only if it is in good health.

Deciding to buy a pet

Many children want to own a pet – especially if a friend has one – and it is often hard for parents to explain why this may not be practical. Bear in mind that children quickly tire of the daily routine of caring for a pet. As the child grows older and moves on to the latest new novelty on the market, the pet sometimes gets neglected. All too often a pet bought for a child ends up being cared for by the parents.

Choosing and losing a pet

Once you and your family have decided to buy a pet, consider its life expectancy and the age of your child at that time. The death of a life-long friend is traumatic for children – as it is for adults. A hamster may live for as little as 2–3 years and its death will almost certainly be an emotional event. Having to put an old or sick pet to sleep is another agonising decision to make. Children may be helped to come to terms with the loss by carrying out a sensitive burial and marking the spot. This way they can relate to where their pet is 'sleeping'.

Find out as much as you can about the chosen pet and read books before you make a purchase. Get to know the animal before purchasing it from a either a reputable breeder, rescue centre or recommended pet shop. Never ever buy a pet from a market or an advert in the newspaper unless there is full documentation with the animal to prove it has been well cared for. Getting a pet from centres such as the RSPCA or Blue Cross ensures that the animal is in good health, fully inoculated and good with children. Giving an unwanted pet a good home is an inexpensive way to pet ownership, and the animal centres need your support.

Animal phobias

If you have a dislike or fear of any animal, try not to let your child know. It is not always easy, but by being frightened yourself, you pass on that fear to your child. Just because in the past you may have had a bad experience with an animal does not mean your child will. No animal will attack or bite unless it is ill, has been mishandled or feels threatened. Never tease or pull an animal. Teaching your child to be aware, cautious and respectful of all animals is the best lesson for your child.

About this book

This book offers parents and children an insight into what happens when you visit the vet with your pet. It also helps give the child an idea of the responsibilities involved when wanting or owning a pet.

First published in 2000 by CP Publishing
Richmond, Surrey, United Kingdom

Text Copyright © 1999 Helen & Clive Dorman
Photographs Copyright © 1999 Helen Dorman
This edition Copyright © 2000 The Children's Project Ltd

Illustrations by Nicky Plumbley

ISBN 1 903275 05 9

Printed in Hong Kong

Acknowledgements

We would like to thank Michael Gilmore's Veterinary Practice in Ham, Richmond, for their help in producing this book. Special thanks to Michael Sadlier, Scott Lackenby, Susan Skelton, Sheila Kemp, Linda Whitehead, Tina Maberley, and to the children, James, Isabelle, Sonny, Fionn, Hattie and Hannah, and of course to the animals.